UNEXPLAINED

ANCIENT MYSTERIES

Rupert
Matthews

QEB Publishing

Project Editor: Paul Manning/White-Thomson Publishing
Designer: Tim Mayer/White-Thomson Publishing
Picture Researcher: Maria Joannou

Published in the United States by
QEB Publishing, Inc.
3 Wrigley, Suite A
Irvine, CA 92618

www.qed-publishing.co.uk

Library of Congress Cataloging-in-Publication Data
Matthews, Rupert.
  Ancient mysteries / by Rupert Matthews.
    p. cm. -- (QEB unexplained)
  Includes index.
  ISBN 978-1-59566-854-7 (library binding)
 1. Civilization, Ancient--Juvenile literature. 2. Curiosities
and wonders--Juvenile literature. 3. Legends--Juvenile
literature. I. Title.
  CB311.M327 2011
  930.1--dc22
                      2010014189

ISBN 978-1-59566-854-7

Printed in the United States

Picture credits
Key: t=top, b=bottom, r=right, l=left, c=center

Bridgeman Art Library Private Collection/The Stapleton Collection
21t, Brooklyn Museum of Art, New York, USA/Charles Edwin Wilbour
Fund 22t, Christopher Wood Gallery, London, UK 26; Corbis Adam
Woolfitt 7b, The Gallery Collection 11, PoodlesRock 16t, Hulton-Deutsch
Collection 25, Homer Sykes 27b; F. Scott Crawford 8b; Getty Images
The Bridgeman Art Library 27t; Library of Congress 8t; Shutterstock
Len Green 2, Eky Chan 3, David Hughes 4b, 21b, Mikhail Nekrasov
5t, Sculpies 5b, 22b, Phillip Minnis 6t, Stargazer 7t, Vitor Costa 8-9
(background), Markus Gann 10t, Jose Ignacio Soto 10b, Tim Arbaev
12b, Jirsak 14, Paolo Jacopo Medda 16b, P.Zonzel 18, Stephen Aaron
Rees 20, Homeros 24b, R_R 28; Stefan Chabluk 6b, 23b; Topham
Picturepoint The Print Collector/HIP 9t, Mike Andrews 12t; Wikimedia
Commons 4t, 19, Andree Stephan 13, Marie-Lan Nguyen 15, Lyndsay
Ruell 17, CaptMondo 23t, Mountain 24t, 31, George Keith 29t,
B Balaji 29b

The words in bold are explained in
the glossary on page 30.

You can find the answers
to the questions asked on
these notebooks on page 31.

CONTENTS

PUZZLES FROM THE PAST

This book is all about ancient mysteries. Some have **baffled** the experts for centuries. A few have been solved, but most have not. Read the evidence and see if you can come up with explanations of your own.

HISTORY OR MYSTERY?

Sometimes a mystery is caused by a simple lack of evidence. Some people think that King Arthur is a fairy story, but others believe that Arthur was a real person who ruled Britain in about the year 500 CE. Unfortunately, in the years that followed the fall of the Roman Empire, nearly all the records of what happened in Britain at that time were lost. The result is that we have no way of knowing if Arthur really existed or not.

Glastonbury in the English county of Somerset is believed to be the place where King Arthur and Queen Guinevere were buried.

Stories about King Arthur are known the world over—but did Arthur really exist?

4

FACTS AND THEORIES

Other ancient mysteries have lasted because so many possible answers could fit the facts. For example, we know that the **pyramids** were built as **tombs** for the **pharaohs** of ancient Egypt. But nobody knows how such huge buildings could have been built by men using only stone and copper tools. **Historians** have plenty of ideas, but no one really knows which theory is right.

The discovery of how to read hieroglyphs has allowed us to find out a huge amount about the ancient Egyptians.

DECODING THE PAST

A few ancient mysteries have been solved with the help of new evidence. For centuries, people knew that Egyptian **hieroglyphs** were a type of writing, but nobody could read them. Then a stone was discovered that had the same messages carved on it in ancient Greek, demotic, and in hieroglyphs. Because experts could understand ancient Greek, they were able to figure out the hieroglyphs. Today, historians can read ancient Egyptian writings easily.

We now know that these giant pyramids were built as burial sites for the Egyptian pharaohs.

TEMPLE OF THE SUN

The mystery of Stonehenge has fascinated people for centuries. This great stone circle is one of the world's most important **prehistoric** sites. But how were the giant stones put in place? Who built it—and why?

Some of the giant stones that form Stonehenge weigh up to 25 tons each. About half were dragged from the Welsh mountains, more than 200 miles (320 kilometers) away.

WHAT IS A HENGE?

A **henge** is a mysterious type of prehistoric monument found in western Europe. It consists of a large round ditch dug into the ground with a bank of earth around it. Most henges have upright stones or wooden posts arranged inside them. Nobody knows what the henges were for, but they would have taken hundreds of people many months to build, so they must have been very important.

A diagram of Stonehenge showing the stone circles and the bank and ditch surrounding the site.

FACTS AND THEORIES

Some think Stonehenge was a temple where people worshipped the sun or the moon. Others think it was a calendar that allowed the people to tell what time of year it was. One recent idea is that it was a place where important local rulers were buried.

STONEHENGE TIMELINE

3100 BCE — Henge earthworks dug.

3000 BCE — Wooden posts erected within the henge.

2600 BCE — "Bluestones" erected.

2400 BCE — Bluestones removed. Huge "Sarsen" stones erected within the henge.

2100 BCE — Bluestones returned.

1600 BCE — Stonehenge abandoned.

WHO BUILT STONEHENGE?

For centuries, people thought that giants or **demons** had built Stonehenge. Then, starting in 1919, **archaeologists** began to **excavate** the area around it.

At certain times of the year, the stones line up with the sun and moon. For instance, the midsummer sun rises over the "Heelstone," while at midwinter the tallest stone lines up with the moon. There are several burial sites in or near Stonehenge. There are also other mounds, ditches, and henges in the area. Although archaeologists have excavated most of these remains, nobody can explain what purpose they served or why they were built.

People who follow ancient religions such as **druidism** still gather at Stonehenge every year to worship nature and celebrate the seasons.

What is a henge?

When were the earthworks first dug?

When was the surrounding area first excavated?

Who were the first Native Americans and where did they come from? Until recently, it was thought they came from Asia via a narrow land bridge with Siberia, but now experts are not so sure.

STONE WEAPONS

Among the earliest known inhabitants of the Americas were the Clovis people. The Clovis were **hunter-gatherers** who lived in North America about 13,000 years ago.

The Clovis people used an unusual type of stone weapon known as the Clovis point, which has a flattened oval shape. These are very similar to weapons that have been found in Europe.

Recently, scientists have found that the **genes** of Native American peoples are very like those of Europeans. This could mean that some of their ancestors originally came to America from Europe, rather than from Asia.

Clovis points were first discovered in the city of Clovis, New Mexico. They have since been found throughout North America and as far south as Venezuela.

MYSTERY FILE
Name Clovis People
Date c.13,000 BCE
Place North America
Status UNEXPLAINED

COINCIDENCE?

Because Clovis points are so similar to stone tools found in Europe, some experts believe that the Clovis people originally came from Europe. It is thought they could have travelled to America via an ice-shelf that once joined the continents.

However, the stone weapons found in Europe stopped being made a thousand years before the time of the Clovis people. Perhaps the similarities between the two are just a coincidence. Nobody knows.

Inuit hunters in the Arctic live by catching fish and hunting animals. If the Clovis people moved westward across the Arctic ice, they may have survived in much the same way.

FACTS AND THEORIES

Climate scientists have discovered that around 15,000 BCE, Arctic sea ice formed a vast land mass stretching as far south as France. This would have made it possible for European people to move westward, living on fish and Arctic animals much like modern Inuit peoples.

When did the Clovis people live in North America?

What is a Clovis point?

How might the Clovis people have reached the Americas?

SECRETS OF THE EGYPTIANS

In recent years, we have found out more and more about the amazing wonders of ancient Egypt. But before experts learned to read Egyptian writing, much of what we know today was surrounded in mystery.

SACRED WRITING

When archaeologists first began to study Egyptian temples and tombs, they found that they were covered with carvings of animals, people, objects, and strange symbols. They knew from ancient Roman writings that the carvings meant something—but what?

The Egyptian symbols carved on this tablet are known as hieroglyphs. The word "hieroglyph" means literally "sacred carving."

In the third millennium BCE, the great Step Pyramid of Dhoser was part of a huge civilization on the banks of the River Nile.

MYSTERY FILE

Name   Egyptian hieroglyphic writing
Date   3200 BCE – 393 CE
Place   Egypt
Status   SOLVED

FACTS AND THEORIES

*In 1824, a French **linguist** and historian, Jean-François Champollion, solved the riddle of the Rosetta Stone. He noticed that certain symbols were enclosed in an oval shape called a **cartouche**. These were names, while the other symbols stood for words, sounds, or ideas.*

THE ROSETTA STONE

In 1799, French soldiers in Egypt found a tablet known as the Rosetta Stone. On it, the same message was carved in Greek, hieroglyphs, and demotic (another type of Egyptian writing). Because experts could read the Greek and demotic, they were able to figure out what the hieroglyphs meant.

The Rosetta Stone dates back to around 196 BCE. Its discovery and later decoding allowed experts to make the first breakthroughs in understanding Egyptian hieroglyphs.

WHAT HAPPENED NEXT?

Since then, thousands of Egyptian texts and carvings have been deciphered, or worked out. These have revealed the entire history of Egypt from about 3200 BCE to 300 BCE. The names of rulers, priests, princesses, and workers have been revealed. We know how Egyptians lived and what they did. The mystery was solved at last.

What is ancient Egyptian writing called?

Who discovered the Rosetta Stone?

Who first decoded the Rosetta Stone?

THE LOST WORLD OF THE MINOANS

From around 2700 to 1450 BCE, Minoan people built a great civilization on the Greek island of Crete. Some of their palaces and temples have survived and are studied by experts. But the greatest Minoan mystery of all is still unsolved....

The carvings on this Minoan clay tablet represent the first written language in Europe.

CLAY TABLETS

In 1900, the archaeologist Arthur Evans discovered more than 2000 clay tablets covered with mysterious **symbols** on the site of the Minoan palace at Knossos in Crete. In ancient times, the tablets would have been left in the sun to dry. Luckily, some were in buildings that had been destroyed in a fire. The fire had hardened the tablets, and so the tablets had survived down the ages.

The tablets showed that the Minoans had created a written language—the first in Europe. But what did it mean?

The palace and temple at Knossos were the center of a civilization that once stretched right across the Aegean.

Evans figured out that the inscriptions were in three different languages: a hieroglyphic script, and two other scripts, which he called simply "Linear A" and "Linear B." When "Linear B" was **deciphered** in 1952, the tablets revealed a lot about the Myceneans, who conquered the Minoans around 1400 BCE.

MYSTERY FILE

Name "Linear A" script
Date 2100–1650 BCE
Place Crete
Status UNEXPLAINED

The Minoans were skilled artists and craftsmen, and Minoan vases and jewelry are among the great treasures of the ancient world.

"Linear A" clearly belonged to a different, earlier language—and since no one knows what language the Minoans spoke, all attempts to decipher the "Linear A" texts have failed.

FACTS AND THEORIES

In 1952, a young Englishman, Michael Ventris, became the first to decipher the tablets found at Knossos on Crete. Ventris discovered that the "Linear B" language was a form of ancient Greek, but the language of "Linear A" is unknown. It may be Iranian, or a type of Phoenician or Greek.

Where was the center of Minoan civilization?

When were the Minoan clay tablets discovered?

What names did Arthur Evans give to the two Minoan scripts?

A WORLD BENEATH THE WAVES

The story of the lost world of Atlantis has fascinated people for centuries. Some believe Atlantis was the site of a very advanced civilization. But could a whole continent and its people *really* disappear beneath the waves?

WHERE WAS ATLANTIS?

The earliest descriptions of Atlantis come from ancient Greek writers, who claimed to have been told all about it by Egyptian priests. According to legend, it was a highly advanced island kingdom, where the people were able to build machines and ships. But if Atlantis really existed, where was the evidence?

MYSTERY FILE

Name	Atlantis
Date	c.9600 BCE
Place	Unknown
Status	UNEXPLAINED

This ruined temple is on the Mediterranean island of Thera, one of many places where Atlantis is said to have been located.

FACTS AND THEORIES

*Recent research into the **eruption** at Thera has shown that it was powerful and highly destructive. Volcanic ash would have plunged much of the Mediterranean into darkness, and the tidal wave that followed would have caused huge damage. Perhaps a disaster this big could have swept away an entire kingdom.*

ATLANTIS TIMELINE

9600 BCE — Traditional date of the destruction of Atlantis.

600 BCE — Greek writers such as Critias learn about Atlantis from Egyptian priests.

360 BCE — The Greek philosopher Plato writes about Atlantis.

One of the most detailed descriptions of Atlantis came from the Greek philosopher Plato (c.427–c.348 BCE).

THE SEARCH FOR CLUES

Some people thought that the Azores in the north Atlantic were the remains of Atlantis. Others preferred Cuba, the Bahamas or the Canaries. By 1900, historians realized that the ancient stories could not be relied on, so they went back to the original evidence to look for clues.

WHAT HAPPENED NEXT?

During the 1950s, archaeologists discovered that around 1550 BCE, the Mediterranean island of Thera had suffered a massive volcanic eruption. An entire city had been destroyed, along with towns on nearby islands. If Atlantis had been destroyed 900 years before the time of the Greeks, instead of 9000 years, then the story might fit!

Who first told Greek writers about Atlantis?

Which island was devastated in about 1550 BCE?

Who wrote a detailed account of Atlantis?

15

CITY OF GOLD

When Spanish people first conquered the Americas in the sixteenth century, many believed there was a city called Eldorado, or the "golden one," waiting to be discovered. But finding it wasn't easy!

MYSTERY FILE

Name   Eldorado
Date   c.1520-1940
Place   South or North America
Status   SOLVED

The historic city of Machu Picchu is the best preserved of all the Inca cities and is now a major tourist attraction.

Led by the soldier and explorer Hernán Cortés, Spanish forces were eager to get their hands on the riches of the Aztec empire of Mexico.

STOLEN GOLD

In 1519, a small force of Spanish soldiers led by Hernán Cortés (1485–1547) accidentally discovered the Aztec empire of Mexico. The Spanish used their modern guns, steel weapons, and armor to conquer the Aztec Indians who lived there. Cortés and his men became very rich on stolen Aztec gold.

INCA TREASURE

In 1532, Francisco Pizarro (c.1471–1541) conquered the even richer Inca empire of South America and stole huge amounts of gold from its people. Spanish explorers began asking about gold wherever they went. Local people told them about a great city filled with gold some distance away. Some said it was to the east, others to the north or south. For years the Spanish searched, but never found it.

Gold was a sacred metal to the Incas and was often used to create beautiful jewelry like this ancient headdress.

FACTS AND THEORIES

Apart from the kingdoms of the Aztecs and Incas, we now know that there was no "golden city" anywhere in the Americas. The most likely explanation is that local people spread rumors about Eldorado in the hope that the Spanish would go away and leave them in peace.

WHAT HAPPENED NEXT?

Later, others took up the challenge. In 1595, the English explorer Sir Walter Raleigh traveled up the Orinoco River in search of a rich city. The Orinoco was explored in 1804, but no city was discovered. In the 1920s, the British adventurer Percy Fawcett set off in search of a lost ancient city in the Amazon rainforest. Neither he, nor the city, were ever found.

Who traveled up the Orinoco River in search of a rich city?

What does the word "Eldorado" mean?

Who led the army that conquered the Aztec Empire?

ISLAND OF STONES

In the Pacific Ocean, thousands of miles from the nearest civilization, lies Easter Island. This strange and mysterious place is famous for its **monumental** stone statues, known as "moai."

A THRIVING COMMUNITY

When Dutch explorer Jacob Roggeveen (1659–1729) first discovered Easter Island in 1722, he found a **thriving** community of more than 3000 people. Yet when a British ship arrived in 1825, her captain, James Cook, found a very different picture: statues had been knocked over and damaged, and many of the island's inhabitants had left, never to return. By 1877, only 111 remained.

"Moai" are huge human figures carved from rock that stare from the hillsides of Easter island. The tallest are almost 30 feet (10 meters) high and weigh around 75 tons.

MYSTERY FILE

Name	Easter Island
Date	1860s
Place	Pacific Ocean
Mystery	SOLVED

MYSTERY COLLAPSE

The mystery of what had happened to the people puzzled historians. How could the community on Easter Island have collapsed, apparently within just 40 years?

WHAT HAPPENED NEXT?

In 1888, when Easter Island was taken over by Chile, historians began to study it to find out what had happened.

Eventually, several answers were found. Too many trees had been cut down, leaving the land exposed to the **elements**. Fighting between different tribes and a massive raid by Peruvian **slave-traders** had also reduced the population.

Arriving at Easter Island in 1825, Captain James Cook found the people hungry and the landscape bleak and bare-looking.

THE ISLAND TODAY

Today, the islanders number just a few hundred. But they still keep their traditions alive and fight to protect the ancient "moai" from further destruction.

FACTS AND THEORIES

*Easter Island was once covered in forests, but in 1600 the last tree was chopped down, and lack of timber soon meant there were no boats left for fishing. The lack of trees also meant that wind and rain removed the topsoil. Crops failed, people went hungry and **disputes** broke out.*

Which Dutch explorer first discovered Easter Island?

Who visited the island in 1825?

How many islanders were left in 1877?

THE LEGEND OF LYONESSE

According to legend, a large and fertile land once stretched from Cornwall in the UK to the Isles of Scilly—until disaster came to Lyonesse one night...

MYSTERY FILE

Name The Lost Land of Lyonesse
Date c.650
Place Under the sea between the Atlantic Ocean and the English Channel
Status DISPROVED

A LAND OF PLENTY

The oldest stories about Lyonesse say that it was a rich farming area that belonged to the King of Cornwall during the time of King Arthur. The land was below sea level, but was protected by a high bank called a dyke. The gates in the dyke were opened at low tide to allow water out, but closed at high tide to stop the sea rushing in.

One night, the man who was supposed to watch the dyke gates decided to go out and enjoy himself with his friends instead. The tide came in, gushed through the open gates and flooded Lyonesse. After the disaster, Cornwall was so poor that it was easily overrun by the English.

The island of St Michael's Mount, off the south coast of Cornwall, has an older name: the "Hill in the Forest." This may be because it was once surrounded by land.

DID LYONESSE EXIST?

In the sixteenth century, Cornish people still referred to the Seven Stones reef off Land's End as the "City of Lions" (Lyonesse). It was also said that you could hear the bells of the drowned city ringing during stormy weather.

The knight Tristram of Lyonesse was a famous hero of Cornish legend.

At very low tides, stone walls and ruined houses can be seen on the seabed off the Isles of Scilly. It is also possible to see the remains of field walls along the sands between Tresco and Sampson. Roman records state that the Isles of Scilly were one much larger island in those days. This area flooded some time between 400 and 1100 CE. Perhaps this large island was the original Lyonesse.

FACTS AND THEORIES

Recent maps of the seabed show that most of the area between Cornwall and the Isles of Scilly is too deep to have been a tidal land. It seems doubtful that Lyonesse ever existed. Perhaps the tales of Lyonesse recall the time before the sea levels rose, 1500 years ago.

The King of Cornwall once ruled his kingdom from the site of this ruined castle at Tintagel on the north coast of Cornwall.

Where was the land of Lyonesse?

Who ruled the land?

Which island has another name meaning "the hill in the forest"?

THE GREAT PYRAMID MYSTERY

The mighty pyramids of Egypt are among the most impressive monuments of all time. For centuries, people have been trying to figure out how they were built without the use of modern tools.

THE GREAT PYRAMID

Of the 138 pyramids in Egypt, the biggest is the Great Pyramid of Giza. It was originally 480 feet (147 meters) tall and 755 feet (231 meters) along each side. Nearly 6.1 million tons (6 million tonnes) of stone were needed to build it. Most of its stones weigh about 2 tons each, but some are up to 91 tons (90 tonnes) in weight.

This carved statue is of the Pharaoh Khufu who ordered the Great Pyramid to be built in c.2571 BCE.

The Great Pyramid is the oldest and largest of the three pyramids at Giza in Egypt. For centuries, it was the tallest building in the world.

FACTS AND THEORIES

*By studying hieroglyphs, experts have learned that the pyramids were tombs of the pharaohs, or rulers, of ancient Egypt. Inside each is a **network** of tunnels and chambers. The pharaoh and his family were buried in the chambers along with furniture, clothes, jewels and food for use in the next life.*

SKILL AND CARE

The pyramid's sheer size is amazing, but so is the skill of the Egyptian builders. The base slopes by only just over half an inch (15 millimeters), and the sides vary by only 2 1/4 inches (58 millimeters). Originally, it was covered with a layer of polished white limestone.

Other pyramids are not so large, but they are just as impressive. It is thought that the pyramid shape was chosen to copy the rays of the Sun striking the Earth.

This is one of the giant stones that once covered the outer face of the pyramid.

STONE ON STONE

Nobody is certain how the pyramids were built. Most people think that the stone blocks were carved in a quarry, dragged on sleds and then hauled into position up a ramp of sand. If so, each pyramid would have taken up to 30,000 men 20 years to build. But no trace of ramps has ever been found.

Another theory is that the stones were dragged up a stone ramp inside the pyramid, but again, no ramp has been found.

King's burial chamber

Queen's burial chamber

Grand Gallery

Entrance

The diagram shows the inside of the Great Pyramid, including the upward-sloping Grand Gallery to the king's burial chamber and the lower route to the queen's.

When was the Great Pyramid built?

What were the pyramids used for?

What was the shape of the pyramids said to copy?

23

THE LEGEND OF TROY

According to Greek **legend**, in about 1250 BCE an army from Greece attacked the city of Troy and destroyed it after a long **siege**. But how much of the legend was based on fact?

STORIES AND POEMS

In ancient times, many stories were told about the Trojan War. The most famous was the **epic** poem the *Iliad*, composed by the Greek poet Homer in around 850 BCE. The Greeks believed that there had been a real Trojan War, though some of Homer's stories were clearly made up.

This golden mask was found at Mycenae by Heinrich Schliemann in 1876. It dates from around the time of the Trojan War and was placed over the face of a king of Mycenae when he was buried.

These remains of the city of Troy are at Hisarlik in modern Turkey.

HISTORY OR MYTH?

By the nineteenth century, people thought that the Trojan War was just a **myth**. Then, in 1870, the German archaeologist Heinrich Schliemann (1822–1890) collected all the clues about Troy and began to dig at a place called Hisarlik in Turkey. What Schliemann discovered showed that Troy could have been a real city after all.

The German archaeologist Heinrich Schliemann always believed that Homer's poem the *Iliad* was based on real events.

FACTS AND THEORIES

Recent research confirms that Troy was a real city. In the 1990s, documents were found that refer to a war between "Taruisa" and Greece. Most experts now agree that "Taruisa"/Hisarlik is Troy, and that the Trojan War was an actual historical event.

MYSTERY FILE

Name	Troy (Illium)
Date	c.1250 BCE
Place	Northwestern Turkey
Status	UNSOLVED

CLUES AMONG THE RUINS

The ruins found by Schliemann showed that the site had been inhabited from around 3000 BCE to around 500 CE. Schliemann found one layer of buildings that had been destroyed by fire. This may have been the city destroyed during the Trojan War, but not everyone is convinced. The built-up area seems to have been too small to be a major city and the defences had curious gaps. Much more work needs to be done at Hisarlik before we have the answers.

When was the Trojan War fought?

Who wrote an epic poem about the Trojan War?

Who first excavated Hisarlik and identified it as Troy?

Over the centuries, many tales have been told about King Arthur of Britain. He is said to have been a worthy knight who ruled over a golden age of peace and plenty. True or not, the stories have certainly stood the test of time.

The young Arthur tries on the crown of Britain. At his side is the magic sword Excalibur.

MYSTERY FILE

Name	King Arthur
Date	c.500 CE
Place	Britain
Status	UNEXPLAINED

KNIGHTS OF CAMELOT

According to legend, King Arthur ruled Britain from Camelot. He led his famous Knights of the Round Table on a series of adventures, including the search for the Holy Grail, the sacred cup used by Jesus at the Last Supper.

At some point, Arthur's nephew Mordred is said to have become envious of his power and begun a civil war. This ended in the death of both men at the Battle of Camlann. After Arthur's death, Britain was plunged into a dark period of war and disaster.

FACTS AND THEORIES

Most of the stories about Arthur that we know today come from a book called the Morte d'Arthur written by Sir Thomas Malory (c.1405–1471). Some historians now think that Arthur really existed, but there is little mention of him in any of the important records of the time.

THE "REAL" ARTHUR?

Around 1150, Geoffrey of Monmouth wrote what is said to be a history of the "real" Arthur. According to Geoffrey, Arthur became ruler of Britain after the Romans left and defeated the invading Saxons at the Battle of Badon Hill, some time between 490 and 517 CE. However, Geoffrey does not say where he got his information. Many think he simply invented it.

This large hill fort known as Cadbury Castle is in the English county of Somerset. Situated close to the river Cam, it is often thought to have been the site of Arthur's court at Camelot.

What was the name of Arthur's castle?

What was the name of Arthur's magic sword?

Who wrote about Arthur in around 1150?

THE SEVEN PAGODAS

With its famous shore temple, Mahabalipuram is one of the most beautiful historic sites in southern India. But if the legends are true, the monuments that survive today are just a fragment of what once existed.

VENGEANCE OF VISHNU

According to an ancient **Hindu** legend, in 550 CE, Hiranyakasipu, the ruler of Mahabalipuram, refused to worship the god Vishnu. His son, Prahlada, wanted to build a temple to Vishnu, and the two argued. Shouting that Vishnu did not exist, the father angrily kicked the shrine that Prahlada had built to Vishnu. Vishnu then appeared and killed Hiranyakasipu.

When Prahlada became ruler, he built seven beautiful **pagodas** that were said to be the finest in all India. The god Indra then became envious of the fine temples to Vishnu and caused six of them to sink into the sea. The surviving temple is known as the Shore Temple.

The shore temple at Mahabalipuram is believed to be one of seven dedicated to the Hindu god Vishnu.

WHAT HAPPENED NEXT?

For many years, the fishermen of Mahabalipuram claimed to see traces of buildings in the sea. Then in 2004, a giant tidal wave called a tsunami struck, shifting banks of sand that had lain undisturbed for centuries. As the seawater retreated, the ruins of buildings began to appear about 1600 feet (500 meters) from the shore.

Archaeologists began digging in the sand and found the ruins of two temples. Under the sea, divers found stone walls and beautiful carvings. Explorations and excavations are still going on to find out if the legendary Seven Pagodas really existed.

This carving of the god Vishnu appears on the wall of one of the temples at Mahabalipuram.

This elephant sculpture at Mahabalipuram is carved out of a single rock.

MYSTERY FILE

Name The Seven Pagodas
Date c.750 CE
Place Mahabalipuram, India
Status UNEXPLAINED

FACTS AND THEORIES

Recent research has found that an earthquake in around 1300 CE caused the land to slip beneath the sea. The shore temple that still stands has been dated to around 750 CE. Nearby are several other temples, but these are much smaller and less impressive.

To which god were the Seven Pagodas dedicated?

Which god is said to have become envious?

What is a tsunami?

29

GLOSSARY

Archaeologist A person who studies the past by looking at buildings, landscapes, and evidence dug up from the ground.

Baffled Confused, very puzzled.

Cartouche In Egyptian hieroglyphics, an oval shape that surrounds the name of a king or queen.

Coat of arms A shield decorated with the badge of a particular person or family.

Commemorate To act as a reminder of a person or a past event.

Decipher To translate from code into a language that everyone can understand.

Demolish To knock down or destroy.

Demon An evil spirit.

Dispute An argument or conflict.

Druidism An ancient religion based on nature worship.

Elements Forces of the natural world, such as sun, wind, and rain.

Epic A type of long poem or story about heroic deeds of the past.

Eruption The pouring out of ash, smoke, and very hot rock from a volcano.

Excavate To dig up from the ground.

Fragment A very small part of something.

Gene A chemical pattern that we inherit from our parents, which makes each of us unique.

Henge A type of prehistoric monument consisting of a circular ditch and bank formed out of earth.

Hieroglyphs An ancient form of Egyptian writing.

Hindu A person who follows Hinduism, a religion that originated in India and is now followed by more than a billion people worldwide.

Historian A person who studies evidence from the past.

Hunter-gatherers People who do not grow crops or keep animals, but obtain food from the land around them.

Legend An old story that has often been told, but that may or may not be true.

Linguist A person who studies languages.

Manuscript A book or document that is written and illustrated by hand.

Medieval The period from the fall of the Roman Empire in the 5th century CE to the fall of Constantinople in 1453 CE.

Miracle An amazing event that cannot be explained.

Monumental Very big or massive, like a large stone statue or building.

Myth An ancient story that is often found not to be true.

Network A system made up of many interconnected parts.

Pagoda A type of eastern temple.

Pharaoh A royal ruler of ancient Egypt.

Philosopher A person who studies the meaning of life.

Prehistoric Very ancient, dating back to a time before writing and record-keeping were invented.

Pyramid A type of huge burial chamber built for the pharaohs of ancient Egypt.

Siege A military operation when an army surrounds a town.

Slave Someone who is forced to work very hard for no money.

Slave-traders People who capture or trade others to be sold as slaves.

Symbol A sign or object that has a special meaning.

Thrive To do well or be successful.

Tomb A burial place or chamber.

ANSWERS

Page

6-7 A prehistoric monument found in western Europe; 3100 BCE; 1919.

8-9 Around 13,000 years ago; a type of stone weapon; via an ice-shelf that joined Europe and America.

10-11 Hieroglyphs; French soldiers in Egypt; the French linguist and historian, Jean-François Champollion.

12-13 On the Greek island of Crete; in 1900; "Linear A" and "Linear B."

14-15 Egyptian priests; Thera; the Greek philosopher Plato.

16-17 "The golden one;" Hernán Cortés; Sir Walter Raleigh.

18-19 Jacob Roggeveen; Captain James Cook; 111.

20-1 Between Cornwall and the Scilly Isles in the UK; the King of Cornwall; St Michael's Mount.

22-3 c.2560 BCE; as tombs for the pharaohs of ancient Egypt; the rays of the Sun striking the Earth.

24-5 c.1250 BCE; the Greek poet Homer; the German archaeologist Heinrich Schliemann.

26-7 Camelot; Excalibur; Geoffrey of Monmouth.

28-9 The Hindu god Vishnu; Indra; a giant tidal wave.

WEBSITES

http://www.caerleon.net/history/arthur/
A comprehensive site covering everything about King Arthur, his life and times.

www.nms.ac.uk/education__activities/
kids_only/egyptian_tomb_adventure.aspx
Join a real-life archaeologist on a mission to explore an ancient Egyptian tomb

http://www.woodlands-junior.kent.sch.uk/
Homework/Greece.html
A website all about Ancient Greece developed by Woodlands Junior School in Kent, UK.

INDEX